WORRY

A Biblical Answer to the King of All Addictions

AMBASSADOR

Printed and Published by
AMBASSADOR PRODUCTIONS LTD,
Providence House
16 Hillview Avenue,
Belfast, BT5 6JR
UK

ISBN   0   907927   92   0

INTRODUCTION

A lady was tossing and turning in her bed one evening. She was worried about her son who had just recently got married. "Why are you worried about him?", said her husband, "He has married a perfectly nice girl who will look after him. Just what are you worried about?"."Oh", she said as she turned yet again in her bed, "I'd be worried if I wasn't worried".

The lady represents a lot of people. Day after day, millions of people waste precious energy and even more precious time focussing their minds on things they have no business trying to deal with or solve or worrying about things that will, in fact, never happen. They charge about with stomachs like spindryers with worry gnawing away in their minds cutting their lifeline to joy and staunching their creativity.

The Bible has a very clear answer to worry. In fact it teaches that worry is a sin, it is a lack of trust in God and His promises. God would have us without anxious care and in this little booklet we want to look at God's way of de-programming the worrier. Is there something overwhelming you at this time? Is there something, bitter as gall, turning you into a frantic individual and stealing your balance in life? Is worry increasing tension in your life to a dangerous level? Here is the Biblical answer to the king of all addictions. May you learn to kick the habit before it kicks you into misery, unhappiness and depression. There is, thank God, a cure available. I trust this little book will help you to apply it.

Derick Bingham.

1. PLENTY TO WORRY ABOUT

Everything today is changing very fast. Computer companies have no sooner put out a new product than they are keeping an even newer one under wraps so that they can sell their present product. We are living in what has been called the "Three Minute Culture". Television advertising tries to sell you as many as four products in three minutes. Twenty years ago, a trade representative on the road wouldn't have dreamt of trying to sell the General Store proprietor four products in three minutes. He would have gone to see him, had a coffee with him, asked him about his family, chatted about a dozen and one things before even getting around to the mere mentioning of his product. Now it's all down to three minutes and the product will sell, not necessarily on its quality, but on the cleverness of its advertising. Cleverness is all.

In the midst of all the hectic pace of modern life, the addiction of worry arises. Under pressure of advertising, people worry that they haven't "made it". Young people worry that they haven't got the right image. The big question of the hour is "are you busy?" If you aren't glancing at your watch to rush on to the next thing, you aren't really living! If you are quietly eating an apple at the side of the street at 3 o'clock in the afternoon, people are inclined to think there is something wrong with you! They almost want you to feel guilty.

Of course frantic living is not the only cause of worry for many people. Unemployment is the other side of the coin. Studies have shown that many people who lose their jobs go through a period of depression. Some get into a vicious circle of declining self- respect, money worries and boredom and they become chronically pessimistic. Reaction to loss of a job is similar to other major losses in life such as the loss of a limb or the death of a loved one. Other worries plague people. All around us there are people facing a broken relationship, or a failed exam, or the frustration of plans foiled by unexpected circumstances. Society around us is drifting into moral chaos and that brings its worries. Old and trusted values are falling. Belief in God is under attack. As E. F. Schumacher has said, "When there are so many gods all competing with one another and claiming first priority and there is no supreme God, no supreme good or value, in terms of which everything else needs to justify itself, society cannot but drift into chaos."[1]

As we look at politics, or the judiciary, or industry or business and commerce, moral values are often swamped with vested interest and people's downright selfishness and ambition. There is a cynicism abroad which would cause anyone to worry. The rise of the occult is also a cause of worry and it has been pointed out that it would probably be safe to say that there are now more witches in England and America than at any time since the Reformation.

And what can we say about the New Age Movement sweeping into Western culture? It is full of pantheism which teaches that there is no distinction between the Creator and His creation. Everything, animate and inanimate is part of a single, impersonal energy called God. "There is", writes Shirley McLaine, the actress, "one basic spiritual law which would make the world a happier and healthier place and it is that everyone is God - everyone". Shirley even takes upon herself the Divine title, "I know that I exist, therefore I am. I know that God exists, therefore it is. But since I am part of that force I am that I am". Such fundamental ego-centricity is blasphemous. It puts the self in the place of God and even declares we are God. New Agers have succumbed to the temptation Satan put to Adam and Eve in the Garden; "You shall be as gods". All around us we see the rise of belief and reincarnation. It also sees Shaminism, which is the art of controlling the spirit world using dreams, visions and "learning to fly within ourselves".

We see the rise of Silva Mind Control which is the transformation of the mind to gain expertise in problem solving involving out-of-body projection during hypnosis. We see Suggestology which is accelerated learning, an accelerated learning method originating in Bulgaria using music and rhymthic breathing. We see Visualisation which is imagining something which one desires in order to achieve it, i.e. changing reality by mental projection. We even have Biofeedback which is the technqiue of controlling normally involuntary bodily functions such as heart-beat or blood pressures to attain a higher awareness of states of consciousness on a scale of 1 (deep sleep) to 8 (cosmic consciousness). Astrologers are on the rise and people are starting to live by what their "stars" say. Such trends are worrying, to say the least.

As we look across the international scene with its wars, its terrorism, its atrocities, its drug trafficking and fraud on a mind- boggling scale, who does not feel worry and fear for the future gripping the mind? What with famines and earthquakes, floods and tornadoes, disasters of all kinds, is there a place where worry can be swopped for inner peace, no matter what the circumstances? Is there a state of equanimity which can face any disturbance? There certainly is and you can find it.

2. WHY WORRY WHEN YOU CAN TRUST?

The scene is a Sunday afternoon in Northern Ireland and quite a stir is being caused. From England and Scotland and from various parts in the Province itself, dozens of people are beginning to converge on the tiny Copeland Islands just off the Northern Ireland coastline. The cause of their interest has not been seen for a hundred and eight years and everyone is determined to, at least, get a glance at it.

What has happened? A white thrush from Russia on a migrating track for Australia has, it seems, been blown off course. Local ornithologists are ecstatic at seeing such a rare appearance in their own back yard.

The greatest teacher who ever lived would certainly not ask us to wait for the rare appearances of foreign birds on our shores before we study our feathered friends. He teaches us that we should constantly consider the birds of the air, if only to learn from them to trust our Heavenly Father and not to have worry-filled lives.

"Therefore I say to you, do not worry about your life, what you will eat or what you will drink; nor about your body, what you will put on. Is not life more than food and the body more than clothing? Look at the birds of the air for they neither sow nor reap nor gather into barns; yet your Heavenly Father feeds them. Are you not of more value than they?" says the Lord Jesus. (Matt. 6: 25-26).

What is Christ saying here about the subject of worry? He is saying that most people are pre-occupied with a trinity of cares; they are primarily concerned with what they will eat, with what they will drink and with what they will wear. People are primarily concerned with the welfare of their bodies. If you doubt Christ's teaching, just lift the nearest magazine or newspaper and have a look at the advertisements. Alternatively, study today's television advertising. What is the theme of these advertisements? Everyone of them is primarily concerned with the welfare of the body. They concentrate on how to feed it, rest it, refresh it, clothe it, entertain it, or titillate it. There is the next exciting novel to read, the present in-place to holiday, the best airline to get you there, the smartest car to drive or the most potent perfume to buy. Here is a page advertising beautiful jewellery or shoes, or whatever, to be an accessory to the best clothes you step out in. The body, though, is the object to which all these advertisements are related. Take the human body away, it seems, and there would be nothing to advertise!

If your body and its comforts is all you are interested in, then Christ is saying yours is a false view of what human beings and human life is all about. If food, clothes and drink is all you are living for, you will get, in going after them, all the worry you can ever hope for, and a lot of ulcers to boot.

You still doubt it? Think then of some young person who has, unfortunately, been recently paralysed or badly hurt in some accident. They will never walk again, or see again, or even move out of bed in their own strength. They cannot even lift a book to read. Now they turn to you and say, "What is life all about?". You say,

"Having a good time". They can't move to have one. "Life is eating lovely food", you answer. They have to get others to feed them. "Life is having wonderful holidays", you suggest. They aren't going anywhere.

"Life is going to see exciting films". They have been blinded.

"Money", you say in desperation, "is the thing to live for". It might buy them a better bed, but is life a better bed?

Physical well-being is not a worthy object for a lifetime's devotion. You are not big enough to be the object of your life. There has got to be more to life or else the longings within us are a mockery. Those who are Christ's disciples know very well that food, drink and clothes, or a pre-occupation with them, is not the supreme goal in life.

The realist, of course, thinks that Christ's teaching is unrealistic. They think Christ is forbidding human beings to use their minds or to plan for the future. If they would consider again His teaching about the birds of the air, they would be aware that He is doing no such thing. What, after all, was our friend, the Russian white thrush doing when it got blown off course to Northern Ireland? Migrating.

No creature plans for the future more than birds do. "Consider them", says Christ. He is not banning human beings from using their minds to prepare for the future. He is not banning thought or forethought, but He is banning anxious thought. Distracting, self-tormenting, corroding, throttling worry is a sin for a Christian.

Christ's argument in this matter is devastatingly logical. "Is not life more than food and the body more than clothing", He argues. Put it this way; were you frightened and worried that you might not live to read the end of this chapter? Of course you weren't. You trusted God to give you life to breathe. In fact you never even think about it, do you?. You always trust Him for it. Well then, if you don't worry about God giving you life every second, why then are you worried all the time about what you're going to eat, about what you're going to drink and about what you're going to wear?

Of course the realists will say that we can't expect God to drop food and clothes and drink from Heaven to us; we have to work for them. So do the birds He asks us to consider. They don't sow and gather harvests into barns like farmers, but they work very hard. God does not feed them in the immediate sense, they actually feed themselves. Some eat seeds, some eat fish, some eat insects, some are predators and others scavenge. God provides in nature all they need to feed themselves. But they are without anxious care about it.

God does the same thing for us. There are ample sources in the earth and sea for everyone. The sad thing is that the selfishness of mankind means that sources are often wasted, or hoarded or spoiled. God has provided for our needs and we need to get out there and work to have them in adequate supply for our homes and families and to help with the needs of others. But we should be like the birds and do it without worry.

And what about plants? Even Solomon in all his glory was not clothed like the lilies of the field, Christ taught. The lilies don't toil like men in a field or spin like women in the house, but they have to draw sustenance from the sun and soil. If God clothes the grass you walk on so wonderfully, which is here today and gone tomorrow, will He not do the same for you? "Oh you of little faith!", says Christ.

Do not for a moment imagine that Christ is saying that His people will not experience trouble. God clothed the grass but it is cut down. God protects sparrows, but they have accidents, can face over-exposure to the cold and they do die, sometimes, of diseases. So it is with people. Wars overwhelm us, accidents strike us in seconds, diseases waste our bodies, trouble erupts in our workplace, unemployment strikes at our pay-packets. It is a fact that God permits suffering. The cross up ahead of the One who taught the truths we are now studying, was going to present suffering above all suffering. Christ did not promise freedom from responsibility, freedom from unexpected circumstances, freedom from complications that baffle, but He categorically promised freedom from worry. All who trust Him can know it.

"Which of you by worrying can add one cubit to his stature?", said the Saviour. The king of all addictions is totally unproductive. Worry won't cure your problems, won't lift and inspire your heart, won't make you easier to live with or won't help those who come across your path. Even worry about tomorrow will make no difference to tomorrow. Today has been given to us and we should get on with what God demands of us today. When tomorrow comes, there will be new troubles, but also renewed strength to face them. There is a touch of humour in the Saviour's advice, is there not, that we should let tomorrow worry about its own things? Today has enough trouble and enough strength from God to get through it.

So it is that feverish worry "amounts to idolatry for its accompanying attachment to mammon means detachment from God. It blurs vision, for, by being pre-occupied with piling up material wealth, it obscures the real goal of our existence, it confuses values, for it attaches primary significance to that which is secondary, and vice-versa as if food were more important than life and clothing than the body. It defies all reason for it barters away heavenly for earthly treasures, the imperishable for the perishable, forgets that it cannot even add one cubit to a person's life-span; borrows tomorrow's troubles as if today's were inadequate; and, worst of all, refuses to consider that if, even as Creator, God feeds the birds and clothes the lilies, then certainly, as Heavenly Father, He will care for His children". 2

What, then is the alternative to worry? The alternative is to trust the Lord and to be pre-occupied with seeking to put His kingdom and His righteousness first in our lives. In our home, in our schooling or university of higher education, in our marriage, in our business, in our professional life, in our part as citizens of the state, in our tax returns or whatever, we must seek to put God and His interests first. God's kingdom exists where Jesus Christ is consciously acknowledged. We must seek at all times to extend that kingdom and if we do, God will take care of our material needs. Having a God-centred life is having a worry-free life; having a self-centred life is to have a worry-packed life. The choice is ours.

It is always good to earth spiritual teaching, as the Saviour did, by practical example. There is a superb example of practical outworking of what Christ is teaching about worry which we can take from the life of that incorrigible Cornish miner and preacher, Billy Bray. Let him tell about the incident himself and may his example inspire us into worry-free living.

Billy was always building new little chapels all over Cornwall and Devon for the worship of God and for the preaching of the Gospel. Billy was very famous for his wit and eccentric sayings and his deep and fervent love for the Lord was respected by many thousands of people. His faith was a very practical faith and in this particular incident concerning the chapel at Kerley Downs, his faith and trust in God truly shines. F. W. Bourne in his book "Glory", a compelling biography of Billy Bray, describes the incident. "When the little place at Kerley Downs was up, Billy began to think where the pulpit could come from. At last, as he looked about among some furniture at an auction sale, his eye fell upon an old three-cornered cupboard. "The very thing!" cried Billy, "The very thing. I can cut a slit down the back of un, and strengthen the middle of un, and put a board up in front of un, and clap a pair o' steers behind un, and then the preacher can preach out of un pretty".

With much glee he turned to someone hear him, and asked, 'What do 'e think they'll want for that there cupboard?' The man looked and gave it is as his opinion that it would go for six shillings. Billy told him what he meant to do with it, and the man said - 'Why, you're Billy Bray. Here, I'll give 'e the six shilling to buy it'.

After a while the cupboard was put up. Billy knew nothing of auctions. All eager to have his pulpit, he cried, holding out his hand - 'Here Mister Auctioneer, here's six shillin' for un; I do want un for a pulpit'. Of course there was a great laugh at Billy's expense. As it passed away the auctioneer cried - 'Six shillings, going for six'. A nod from behind Billy was quickly caught. 'Seven,' said the auctioneer, 'seven shillings.'

'No,' cried Billy, ''tis only six; there's the money.' Of course, down went the hammer and much to Billy's astonishment, the cupboard was not his.

'Well, Father do know best,' said he in a rather disappointed tone; but anyhow I must give the man back his six shilling.'

The man was gone, nor was Billy likely to see him again. This was a new and even greater trouble.

'I'll be gone down and tell Father about it,' said Billy, as he started off for his little chapel.

With faith renewed, and a comfortable assurance that it would be all right, he was coming from the chapel, when he saw the cupboard going up the hill in a cart. 'I'll follow un, anyhow,' he whispered,'an' see the end.' They carried it to a house, and tried to take it inside, but it was just too big to get in. They twisted and turned, they pulled and pushed, but it was no use.

'Here's a mess,' said the purchaser angrily; 'I've given seven shilling for un, an' shall have to skat un up for firewood.'

Then, as his eyes twinkled, Billy stepped over and put his hand on the man's shoulder as he stood, hat in hand, wiping his forehead. 'I'll give 'e six shillin' for un, if you'll carry un down to my little chapel.'

'That I will,' said the man, pleased at being so well out of it.

'Bless the Lord!' cried Billy, ''tis just like Him, He knew I couldn't carry un myself, so He got this man to carry un for me. 3

3. WHY WORRY WHEN YOU CAN PRAY?

The scene is Philippi in Macedonia, famed scene of the decisive battle in which armies loyal to the murdered Julius Caesar, fighting under the joint command of Octavian and Mark Anthony, defeated the rebel forces of Brutus and Cassuis. Now enlarged, the city, named after the father of Alexander The Great, has been given the "Ius Italicum" which represents the legal quality of Roman territory in Italy -

the highest privilege obtainable by a provincial municipality. Philippi is a colony of Rome and its people could purchase and own or transfer property and have the right to civil law suits. They are exempt from both the poll tax and are proud of it.

The Gospel of Jesus Christ slips into the city of Philippi in ever so quiet a fashion. The Gospel also slips on to the Continent of Europe for the first time. It is interesting to note that the first sermon preached is given, not standing up, but sitting down. No fanfare or public relations experts preceded it, no advertising campaign makes the people aware of the life-changing nature of what is about to invade their lives and cultures. Paul, the great Christian Apostle, in Philippi for the first time, finds some Jewish women holding a prayer meeting down on a river bank. He sits down among them and speaks of Christ. A business woman called Lydia has a conversion experience as he talks. "The Lord", says Scripture, "opened her heart". Lydia then opens her home to the Apostle and his friends, Timothy, Silas and Luke, and the Lord opens Philippi and a Continent to His Gospel.

It is fascinating to meditate on the fact that Lydia's heart was God's highway to Europe. Soon a Philippian jailer is converted in earthquake circumstances and a Christian Church begins to meet in Lydia's home.

One memorable day, a letter arrives for the young Church at Philippi, written by Paul. Of all the letters he wrote, this is to prove to be, unquestionably, the happiest. It may have been written for more or less personal reasons, but inspired of the Holy Spirit, everything in it has a universal application, even to our circumstances today. The laws of the spiritual life never change. This is why the advice given in this amazing letter is as applicable today as it was when it was first written. This is why the Bible is of such vital importance in the life of the christian; every conceivable experience which the christian may have to face has already been met and dealt with somewhere in the Scriptures. Here then is an astonishing and remarkable letter.

This theme of the Philippian letter is a very contagious subject. Sixteen times the word "joy" and its derivitive "rejoice" is mentioned. Victory in Christ is bringing joy to Paul's life like nothing else ever has. He writes that the One who has begun a good work in the Philippian christian's lives will finish it. Mankind might leave unfinished temples and abandoned projects. Artists may leave unfinished pictures, entrepreneurs may leave unfinished business plans but the One who creates a desire for God in us, reveals the work of Christ and the real meaning of Calvary to us, forgives our sins and creates new life in us, goes on to make us more like Christ through all the circumstances of life.

Paul underlines the fact that he will go on doing it "until the day of Jesus Christ" (Philippians 1; 6). What does this mean? It means that until the day when there will be "a new heaven and a new earth in which righteousness dwells" and Christ will return to reign as King, God will continue to work in a christian's life knocking off the rough edges and making us more like the Lord Jesus. It is a formidable task. "How on earth do you do it?", said someone to the sculptor as he faced a huge block of marble out of which he had to carve a horse. "Everything that does not look like a horse has to go!", he replied quietly.

So it is that everything that is not Christlike in the believer's life has to go: that is God's continual aim as He works in a christian's life. This confidence in God's continuing work in the life of the christian is the basis of Paul's incorrigible joy. Joy, you see, is not a feeling so much as it is an attitude.

It is an equanimity of spirit which is not determined by people, or circumstances, or possessions or lack of them. With most people, if their circumstances are overwhelming, they too are in chaos of mind and spirit. Not Paul. He writes to the Philippian christians while under house arrest, quite possibly chained to a soldier on either wrist, and certainly with no privacy from dawn to dusk, from the midnight hour to the cock crowing. The man who writes of joy and contentment is facing trial before a notorious Emperor called Nero who might have him beheaded at any time. Yet, he is at peace!

If you think your circumstances are bad; try these. "From the Jews five times I received forty stripes minus one. Three times I was beaten with rods; once I was stoned; three times I was shipwrecked; a night and a day I have been in the deep. In journeys often, in perils of waters, in perils of robbers, in perils of my own countrymen, in perils of the Gentiles, in perils in the city, in perils in the wilderness, in perils in the sea, in perils among false brethren; in weariness and toil, in sleeplessness often, in hunger and thirst, in fastings often, in cold and nakedness - besides the other things, what comes upon me daily, my deep concern for all the churches". (2 Corinthians 11; 24-28). It is quite obvious that lashings cannot beat the joy out of Paul's life, weary travelling in wilderness country cannot dry up his joy, false christians cannot poison his joy, cold weather and exposure cannot freeze it, and burning sun cannot wither it.

These are not the musings of some ivory tower sophisticate who doesn't live in the nitty gritty of life; this is a man who speaks truth right out of the cauldron of reality. There is in his life a distinct absence of the things that make life comfortable, yet Paul doesn't lose his joy. He doesn't moan, "Why does God allow these things?", nor does he become soured and embittered and turn his back upon Christ and His Church. He is confident, even though a victim. He is joyful, in spite of others. He is hopeful, regardless of uncertainty. He is contented because Christ is central to his life. For him to live is Christ and to die is more of Christ.

Why is he, though, not eaten up with worry? Couldn't he be allowed to worry, just a little? With everything seemingly against him, how could this man survive with such a calm, contented spirit? How can any christian survive without worry? Paul lets the Philippians know his secret and his secret can be ours. He puts it in one incredible sentence.

"Be anxious for nothing", he writes, "but in everything by prayer and supplication with thanksgiving, let your requests be made known to God and the peace of God which surpasses all understanding will guard your heart and mind through Christ Jesus". (Philippians 4; 6-7). In this simple, powerful sentence lies the cure to the king of all addictions. In the light of it, if applied to your life, it will make worry flee.

What is worry? It is, according to the dictionary, "to be unduly concerned". It comes from the German word "wurgen" which means to strangle, to choke". Worry very quickly becomes the dictator of how you feel and react to your circumstances, mentally harassing you, emotionally stringing you out and spiritually strangling you. A worry can be defined as anything that drains your life of joy. What then is Paul telling us in Philippians 4; 6-9? He is saying, "Worry about nothing and pray about everything". He is saying to all of us, "Switch everything from your worry list to your prayer list". He is calling us to let God know what is troubling us. He is saying, in effect, that prayer is a conversation with, a plea directed to, a request made of, information given to the supreme Person of the Universe who can hear, know, understand, care about and respond to the concerns that otherwise would sink us in despair.

But notice that the real accent of this amazing sentence of Paul's is that prayer is to be given with thanksgiving. As Barth put it, "To begin by praising God for the fact that in this situation, as it is, He is so mightily God - such a beginning is the end of anxiety. To be anxious means that we ourselves suffer, ourselves groan, ourselves seek to see ahead. Thanksgiving means that giving God the glory in everything, making room for Him, casting our care upon Him, letting it be His care.

The troubles that exercise us then cease to be hidden and bottled up. They are, so to speak, laid open to God, spread out before Him".

If we do this, what ensues? The peace of God will be ours. The expression, "The peace of God" found here is found nowhere else in the New Testament. It isn't peace with God, that we have already when we are justified by faith in Christ, such peace is pre-supposed. It is the tranquility of God's own eternal being, the peace which God Himself has - the calm serenity that characterises God's very nature and which christians are welcome to share. This peace of God will, according to Scripture, pass all understanding. What does this mean? It means it is able to produce better results than human planning. It is far superior to any person's schemes for security. It is more effective for removing anxiety than any intellectual effort or power of reasoning.

Think about this. If you were to gather every brilliant mind from the universities of your country, from the Government of your country, from the schools of your country and set them to solve the particular problem which is worrying you today, prayer will bring a peace in your circumstances which will far surpass all that these minds could come up with! It "rises above" all understanding.

There are certain questions we have in life which are not answered for us. Like Job, we do not know why we are going through certain alarming difficulties in our lives, but God, although He has not explained the situation, has promised us that He will give us sufficient grace to enable us to go through. It is part of our discipline sometimes to be kept in ignorance to be shown that we are finite and the important thing is not so much what happens to us as our attitude to what happens. Prayer transforms our attitude and immediately we start praying, a calm confidence and the experience of the peace of God will supplant worry and anxiety. Scripture promises that as a result of prayer, God's peace will flood your life. Try it; it beats worry, any day. As for the nightime, just hand those worries to God in prayer before you go to bed tonight. Why? Because He is going to be up all night anyway, isn't He?

4. WHY WORRY WHEN YOU HAVE A GUIDE?

I had a question for him. His name was Mr. Neville Taylor, decorated by the French Government for, among other things, his very dedicated work of translating the Scriptures into the Mbai language of the Tchad. "How did you translate the verse in Isaiah 26; 3?" I asked him. It is a verse which speaks of how a person is kept in perfect peace whose mind is stayed on God. "We translated it that God would keep the person's heart 'lying down' whose mind was stayed on Him," Neville answered. My mother was dying and coming home from school-teaching one day, I remember very well laying my books down at the bottom of her bed and looking her straight in the eye and, loving her very much, I gently asked what it meant to be a Christian when one had to go through what my dear mother was suffering. "Do you see that text on the wall?", she said. It read, "Thou will keep him in perfect peace whose mind is stayed on Thee". "I had a friend", she said, "who was a missionary in China and the local dialect which she spoke had that verse say, "Thou will keep him in perfect peace whose mind stops at God".

I love those two stories of two translations of Isaiah's famous verse because they perfectly sum up all that God does for the worried mind that rests on Him. The Scriptures are actually calling us to take our minds beyond the immediate worry of our lives and rest them on the God of our lives. So, don't let your mind stop at your worry; let is stop at God. It really does make a difference. It will result in a heart that, as the Mbai folk would say, "lies down".

As you let your mind stop at God, then His character and attributes become more and more relevant to you. One of those great attributes is that God is our Guide. "He leads me beside the still waters...... He leads me in the paths of righteousness for His Name's sake", writes King David. What does that mean? It means that if God does not guide you, then His very Name and its worth are at stake. How many advertisements do you see in modern life with the phrase attached, "and that's guaranteed"? God's Name, reverently speaking, is His guarantee. He is not on probation, either, nor does He have to pass an examination. His Name is to be trusted, not put on probation.

There is no greater cure for worry than the promise of the guidance of God. It is not, though, that it is always easy to understand, is it?

Let's think about three incidents in Scripture on the subject of the guidance of God for our help.

Take the disciples on the lake, for example. It is dark and "Jesus was not come to them" (John 6; 17). Their little vessel is plunging and lunging in a heavy storm and they have rowed for over three hours and have only covered about three miles. Where is their Master? At a prayer meeting with His Father on a mountain. There is no sign of Him coming to the aid of His worried and frightened disciples. Where is the God who promises to lead them, now?

The second example concerns a very cultured character called Jairus. With great courage he has identified with Christ by falling at His feet and pleading with Him to come and help his dying daughter. Jesus turns to go with Him but as He passes through the crowd, an anonymous woman touches the fringe of His robe. Our Lord not only takes time to hear some of the thronging people deny having touched Him, He takes time to wait for the woman to confess to it. There is no sense of hurry as He stays to pronounce a blessing upon her in the hearing of the crowd. While Jesus lingers, speaking to the woman, messengers come from the house of the synagogue ruler to say that any further appeal to Jesus is of no use; his little daughter has died. Can you imagine how Jairus felt in that circumstance? What is the Lord, who leads and guides His people, doing with him now? The delay of the Lord Jesus must have seemed extremely strange.

The third case concerns Christ's closest friends, Mary, Martha and Lazarus. One might, outwardly, have seen the reason why Jesus delayed in going to help the storm-tossed disciples (prayer) or Jairus' daughter (a fellow sufferer) but the delay in visiting his very sick friend Lazarus was deliberate (See John 11: 5-7). Then, when Lazarus died, the Lord took His time, deliberately, on the journey to Bethany. How do we know? The answer is very straightforward. From Betharba where Christ was at the time, to Bethany where Lazarus lived, was about two days distant by foot; so, the Lord could easily have got to Bethany before Lazarus' illness had given place to death. Even, after that, He evidently lingered on the journey for when He reached Bethany, the Bible tells us that Lazarus had already been four days in the tomb! Friend and all as Christ was to Mary, Martha and Lazarus, deliberate delay in coming to their aid seems incredibly strange.

Was God guiding in all these delays? Of course. He delayed with the disciples in the storm because he wanted to teach them that He had power over nature. He came, in His perfect timing and calmed the waters. He delayed to visit Jairus' daughter to prove to Jairus that He not only had power over disease, He also had power over death. Mary and Martha both scolded Christ for not being at hand on time; they both said on separate occasions, "Lord, if you had been here, my brother would not have died". Imagine scolding the One who has never allowed a planet to be late yet, never mind Himself!

Christ, of course, delayed in order to show them, among other things, that not only had He power over nature or death, He had power over decomposition. Christ raised the already decomposing body of Lazarus from the tomb. His delays always become His delights.

We must never worry when God delays to resolve a situation. All things that happen to us are not good but they work together for good. Always. He will not leave you guideless, Christian. You are no longer lost, you have been found by the Good Shepherd and He is always leading you on to further and better things.

Did Joseph think God was guiding when he was thrown into a pit by his brothers? Did Moses think God was guiding when Pharoah threw him out of Egypt? Did Hannah think God was guiding when she was childless? Did Elisha think God was leading when Jezebel lifted her tongue against him? Did Daniel and his friends think God was guiding when three of them were thrown into a fiery furnace and Daniel himself into a den of lions? Did Jonah think God was leading when he arrived in the great fish's stomach? They certainly wondered, but God was leading them all the time; just like He is leading you. I put it this way once in a little poem.

> Just as he was having his toughest day,
> And Goliath was coming with a lot to say,
> And Israel was silent, come what may,
> God was working it out for good!
>
> Just as they thought it would never come,
> And three walls surrounded Babylon,
> And the people of God were sick for home,
> God was working it out for good!
>
> Just when the times were dark and dread,
> And the Assyrian hosts by a fiend were led,
> The angel moved and the foe lay dead,
> God was working it out for good!
>
> Just when they thought their case was lost,
> They heard a knock and said, "It's a ghost",
> But Peter arrived when they needed him most,
> God was working it out for good!

Just stop today and bow your knee,
Though you're ready to scream and ready to flee,
Lift your heart to Him and say with me,
God is working it out for good!

Why should you worry when you have such a guide? You shouldn't. I think of the famous singer and teenage idol, Michael Jackson, with a ranch of 125,000 acres and millions of dollars in the bank. "What are you sure of, Michael?", asked the T.V. presenter, Ophra Winfrey. "I'm not sure of anything", answered Michael. Tragically sad words, aren't they? A christian could never say such a thing, for christians are sure of home. They have believed and "are persuaded that He is able to keep that which they have committed to Him against that day". The emphasis is not just on WHAT Christians believe but upon WHOM they believe. Got it? Not "what" so much as "whom". He can be trusted to guide us and keep us until the very end of life.

It is a fact that the biggest tests in life do not come while you are young; they come when you are coming nearer the end of life. Satan doesn't tempt the older Christian with things he puts across the path of the younger Christian. Why? Because the older Christian knows such seemingly attractive pathways are only, in the end, unsatisfying cul-de-sacs. Satan comes to older Christians, now losing their friends and facing pain and suffering and loneliness and says, "Where is your God now?" Worry could swamp such people until they realise that the younger generation are looking to them to display what it is like to be a Christian in such circumstances. How much harder it is to face pains and aches and loneliness and difficulties without worry, and ultimately, to face, if the Lord be not come, death itself. But it can be done with such a Guide as ours.

Let me close this little book with a story from my own local church that succinctly describes how worry can be overcome, even when facing death. An elder in my local church, a Godly man called Mr. Ross Pinkerton was for quite a few years a lamplighter in the Stranmillis area of Belfast. He set out at dusk each night to light the dozens of gas lamps in his district and he told me of how, as a lamplighter, he made so many friends on his route. Children would talk to him, adults would even come out of their houses and tell him their troubles. An hour before dawn, each morning, Mr. Pinkerton would set off again to put all the gas lights out.

When describing this work to me, once, he slipped in a little gem of spiritual truth. He told me that a lamplighter was once asked if he did not get awfully frightened in the dark as he set out to put out the lights. "No", he replied smiling, "When one light goes out, I keep my eye on the next one and by the time the last one is out, it is morning!"

So christians have the promise of Scripture that they will, all their days, walk in the light, no matter how dark their circumstances. God's lights of guidance are always ahead. Even when facing death, it is but the valley of the shadow and there cannot be a shadow without a light. There is even a light in the valley of death! Then it will be the dawn of eternal day. If the Lord is your light and your salvation, of whom shall you be afraid? No-one. With such a Guide, you need not even worry. Never, ever.

REFERENCES

1. E. F. Schumacher, "A Guide for the Perplexed".(Jonathan Cape, 1977), T.69.
2. "Matthew", William Hendriksen. New Testament Commentary.Banner of Truth Trust. Page 343.
3. "Glory", The Biography of Billy Bray by F. W. Bourne.Page 62-63. Ambassador.

Derick Bingham is a Bible teacher with the
Crescent Church, Belfast. The following is a selection of
message tapes from "Tuesday Night at the Crescent"

JOY - THE CHRISTIAN'S SECRET STRENGTH
A study of Paul's letter to the Philippians

Confidence: The basis of joy
Tough Circumstances: The test of joy
Consistency: The progress of joy
Christlikeness: The completion of joy
Self: The enemy of joy
Friends: The fellowship of joy
Pride: The killer of joy
Principle: The anchor of joy
Citizenship: The mark of joy
Harmony: The music of joy
Worry: The disturber of joy
Contentment: The fruit of joy
Power: The fuel of joy

HOME, WHERE LIFE MAKES UP ITS MIND

Is family life facing extinction?
What is God's blueprint for marriage?
Is monogamy God's will?
Is marriage God's plan for everyone?
The most unpopular requirement for marriage
Are we undertaking marriage too lightly?
Is marriage worth waiting for?
Why do couples fight?
Don't be a passive parent
How should we discipline our children?
Living with teenagers
When the unbearable is inescapable
Tell debt do us part
Commitment is the key

THE RELUCTANT HERO
A study of the life of Moses

Born after midnight
Lessons learned from failure
Burning bridges or bushes
Lord here am I, send Aaron!
When they all stand up against you
Plaques that preach
The night nobody slept
Between the devil and the deep Red Sea
Is the Lord testing you?
Giving up a good thing for a better
Reverence, the forgotten attitude
The believers occupational hazards
What bad temper can do
Do shadows frighten you

THERE IS AN ALTERNATIVE

Studies in the Sermon on the Mount

The most radical lifestyle, ever
The richest self-fulfilment possible
How to make life tasty
Overcoming anger and lust
Divorce and oathtaking: are they permissible?
Should we turn the other cheek?
How to love your enemy
Beware! Religious performance now showing
Are you into prayer and fasting
The tragedy of Mr Facing Bothways
Are you a worrier?
Putting an end to labelling people
The narrow way doesn't get broader
The simple secret of an unsinkable life
The amazing Lord Jesus

DOES GOD STILL GUIDE?

Biblical principles on knowing God's will for your life

Guidance: Why do we need it?
Guidance: When does it come?
Guidance: How do we know it?
Guidance: Can we stray from it?
Guidance: Does prayer affect it?
Guidance: Why is it often delayed?
Guidance: So, what about it?

THE ROAD LESS TRAVELLED BY

A study of Christ's influence in life's decisions

When you are facing temptation
When you are facing misunderstanding
When you are facing doubt
When you are facing inadequacy
When you are facing pain
When you are facing disqualification
When you are facing shame
When you are facing success addiction
When you are facing a need for grace

Audio cassettes are £3:00 each
(add 25p post and packing)
Available from :-
Ambassador Productions Ltd.
16 Hillview Avenue
Belfast BT5 6JR
Northern Ireland